HOOPS

Robert Burleigh

Illustrated by Stephen T. Johnson

For John the Playmaker, Buckets, Fleetline,
Collella, Diz, Bobby the Dealer, Hus, Doctor B.,
Heidi who took 'em by surprise, Gene the Machine,
Francisco Bang-Bang, Razz and the Rapman, Diego,
Smooth Teddy, Jerry and Harry, the two Mikes, and
all the lads who ever laid rubber to cement in
O'Keeffe Playground: "Go up strong!"

--R. B.

For Joni,
with special thanks to Jackson, Jamal, Matt,
Peter, Sean, Stephen, and Tom

--S. T. J.

Text copyright © 1997 by Robert Burleigh
Illustrations copyright © 1997 by Stephen T. Johnson

Silver Whistle is a trademark of Harcourt Brace & Company.

Library of Congress Cataloging-in-Publication Data
Burleigh, Robert.
Hoops/Robert Burleigh; illustrated by Stephen T. Johnson.
p. cm.
"Silver Whistle."
Summary: Illustrations and poetic text describe the movement
and feel of the game of basketball.
ISBN 0-15-201450-0
1. Basketball--Juvenile poetry.
(1. Basketball--Poetry. 2. American poetry.)
I. Johnson, Stephen, 1964- ill. II. Title.
PS3552.U7255H66 1997
811'.54--dc20 96-18440

First edition

F E D C B A

Printed in Singapore

The illustrations in this book were done in pastels on Ingres paper.
The display type was set in Mystery Black.
The text type was set in Typewriter Bold.
Color separations by United Graphic Pte Ltd., Singapore
Printed and bound by Tien Wah Press, Singapore
This book was printed on totally chlorine-free Nymolla Matte Art paper.
Production supervision by Stanley Redfern and Pascha Gerlinger
Designed by Kaelin Chappell and Stephen T. Johnson

Hoops.
The game.
Feel it.

The rough roundness.
The ball
like a piece
of the thin long reach
of your body.

The way it answers whenever you call.
The never-stop back and forth flow,
like tides going in, going out.

The smooth,
skaterly glide
and sudden swerve.

The sideways slip
through a moment of narrow space.

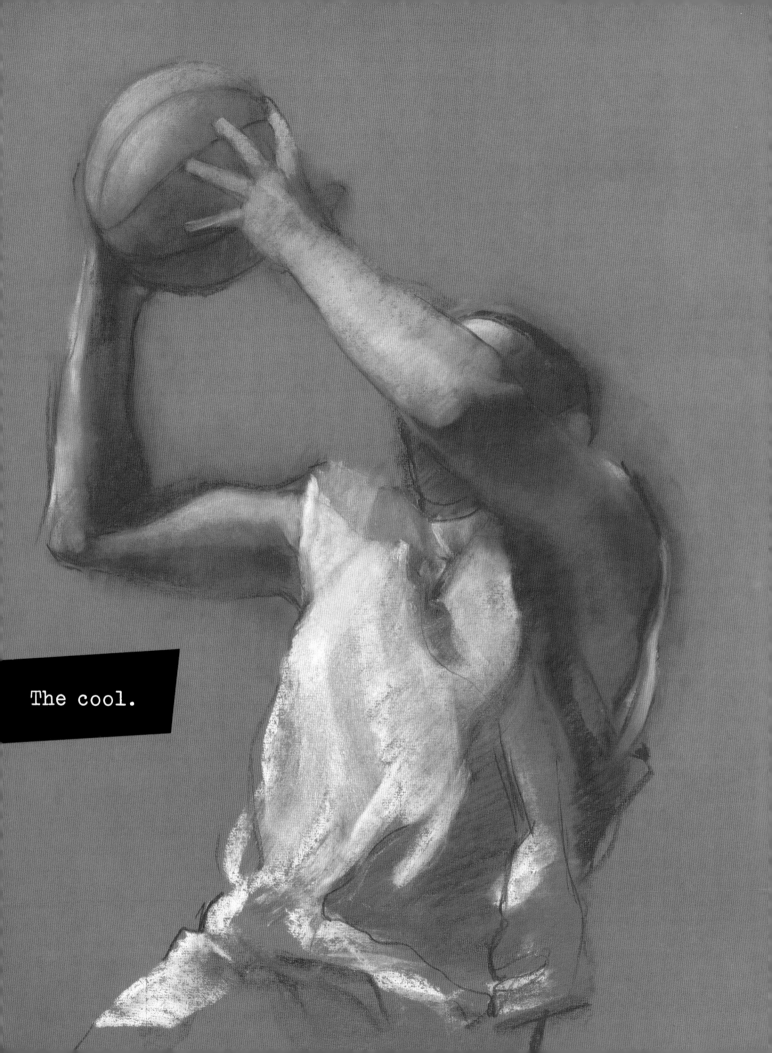

The cool.

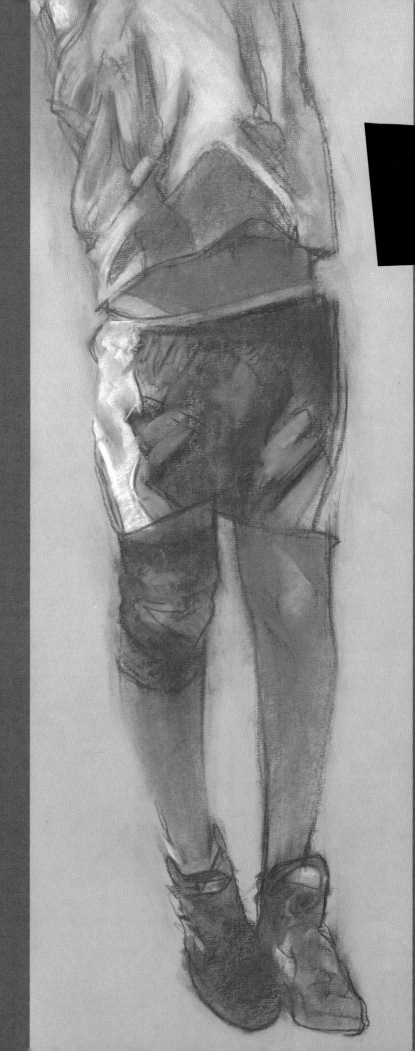

The into
and under
and up.

The feathery fingertip roll
and soft slow drop.

Feel your throat on fire.

Feel the asphalt burning beneath your shoes.

The two-of-you rhythm.

The know-where-everyone-is without having to look.

The watching
and waiting
to poke
and pounce.

The fox on the lurk.

The hunger.

The leap from the pack.

The out-in-the-clear
like a stallion
with wind in your face.

The bent legs tense
as the missed shot swirls
and silently spins.

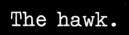
The hawk.

Your arm shooting up
through a thicket of arms.

The lean
and brush
and burst free.

The skittery,
cat-footed dance
along the baseline.

The taste
for the rock in your hands
when it counts the most.

The weight of you
hanging from fine,
invisible threads.

The eyes.

The arc.
The no-sound
sound of the ball

as it sinks
through nothing but still,
pure air.
Yes.

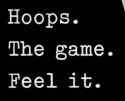
Hoops.
The game.
Feel it.